Handy Idaho Genealogy Handbook

I0439897

Gary L. Morris

ISBN-13: 978-1508404149

ISBN-10: 1508404143

Table of Contents

Notes

Genealogical Research in Idaho

Idaho is the thirteenth largest state in the U.S. and is famous for the many gemstones found there. There are also many historical and genealogical gems to be found in Idaho, but don't worry; you won't have to dig too much for them, we'll show you exactly where they are. To get you started in tracing your Idaho ancestry, we'll introduce you to those records, and help you to understand:

1.   What they are
2.   Where to find them
3.   How to use them

These records can be found both online and off, so we'll introduce you to online websites, indexes and databases, as well as brick-and-mortar repositories and other institutions that will help with your research in Idaho. So that you will have a more comprehensive understanding of these records, we have provided a brief history of the "Gem State" to illustrate what type of records may have been generated during specific time periods. That information will assist you in pinpointing times and locations on which to focus the search for your Idaho ancestors and their records.

A Brief Genealogical History of Idaho

Idaho has a very colourful, multi-cultural history. It is believed that Native Americans have lived in Idaho for over 14,000 years. Before the arrival of Mexican and European explorers, it is believed that approximately 8,000 Native Americans inhabited the area. The major tribes that inhabited the area were the Shoshone, Nez Perce and Kootenai.

Spanish explorers ventured into the area starting in 1592 and introduced domestic fowl, pigs, tomatoes, corn, beans, and garlic to the natives. When Lewis and Clark entered the area during their famous search for a navigable route to the Pacific Ocean, they encountered Spanish speaking Native Americans. Following Lewis and Clark, French-Canadian fur trappers flocked to the area. Their influence is reflected in the French names of communities such as Boise and Coeur d'Alene. The fur trade in Idaho employed many Hawaiian islanders as labor, and when Fort Boise was established in 1834, nearly the entire staff was from the Hawaiian Islands.

Many Spaniards and Mexican also lived off the land as hunters and trappers, and by 1863 the Mexicans were operating a mine at Spanish Town, a small settlement near Rocky Bar. One of the most successful Mexican businessmen in Idaho during this time was Jesus Urquides. He built a profitable packing company, and established a settlement known as the Spanish Village in the 1870's to house his Mexican workers. There were 60 Mexican born individuals recorded in the 1870 census.

Later in time African Americans came to the area in order to trap, trade, and work the mines. Many of those who came before the Civil War were escaped slaves, but after the Civil War, and with the railroad entering Idaho in the 1880's, many African Americans settled in Pocatello. There were also four companies of troops from an African-American unit the 24th Regiment sent to Idaho in 1899. Many stayed after finishing their service, and the 1900 Idaho census showed 940 African Americans living there.

Idaho's population during the Gold Rush of the early 1800's was one quarter Chinese, and by 1870, almost every miner was Chinese.

At one time, during the Gold Rush of the early 1800s, Idaho's population was one-quarter Chinese. By 1870, a majority of all Idaho miners were Chinese. The mid 1800's saw many settlers flocking to the western states to flee from religious or political persecution. One such group was the Mormon's, while many Union and Rebel supporters flocked there to escape the Civil War.

During the 1890s, several thousand Japanese laborers were working in Idaho to construct the railroad, while between 1900 and 1920; a large population of Basque immigrants from the Pyrenees came to Idaho to work as sheepherders.

Between 1900 and 1920 a large number of Basque immigrants came to Idaho from the Pyrenees to work as sheepherders. Today, Boise boasts the largest Basque community in the entire United States.

Important Genealogical Dates in Idaho History

1818 – United States and Great Britain occupy the area by treaty

1834 – Fort Hall built on the Snake River by fur traders

1843 – Falls under the laws of the Oregon territory

1846 – 49th parallel adopted as the border between British North America and the United States

1848 – Officially recognized as part of the Oregon Territory

1853 – Northern Idaho becomes part of the Washington Territory

1859 – Southern Idaho becomes part of the Washington Territory

1860 – Mormon settlement established at Cache Valley, gold discovered at Orofino Creek

1863 – Created as a separate territory from Washington

1866 – Snake War

1890 – Statehood

Famous Battles Fought in Idaho

Idaho has a relatively peaceful history, though there were famous skirmishes between U.S. troops and the Native American tribes in what was known as the **Snake War**. The battle accounts can be very effective in uncovering the military records of your ancestor. They can tell you what regiments fought in which battles, and often include the names and ranks of many officers and enlisted men.

Snake War:
http://www.3rd1000.com/history3/events/camplyon.htm

Common Idaho Genealogical Issues and Resources to Overcome Them

Boundary Changes: Boundary changes are a common obstacle when researching Idaho ancestors. You could be searching for an ancestor's record in one county when in fact it is stored in a different one due to historical county boundary changes. The **Atlas of Historical County Boundaries** can help you to overcome that problem. It provides a chronological listing of every boundary change that has occurred in the history of Idaho.

Atlas of Historical County Boundaries:
http://publications.newberry.org/ahcbp/documents/ID_Consolidated_Chronology.htm#Consolidated_Chronology

Name Changes: Surname changes, variations, and misspellings can complicate genealogical research. It is important to check all spelling variations. Soundex, a program that indexes names by sound, is a useful first step, but you can't rely on it completely as some name variations result in different Soundex codes. The surnames could be different, but the first name may be different too. You can also find records filed under initials, middle names, and nicknames as well, so you will need to **get creative with surname variations** and spellings in order to cover all the possibilities. For help with surname variations read our instructional article on **How to Use Soundex**.

get creative with surname variations:
http://obituarieshelp.org/blog/?p=634

How to Use Soundex: http://obituarieshelp.org/blog/?p=505

Idaho Genealogical Organizations and Archives

Genealogical resources include not only records, but the organizations that house them, or can direct you to them. These institutions include: *Archives, Libraries, Genealogical Societies, Family History Centers, Universities, Churches, and Museums.*

Following are links to their websites, their physical addresses, and a summary of the records you can find there.

Idaho Archives

National Archives—Pacific Alaska Region (Seattle) – Federal census records, military records, passenger lists, naturalizations, Native American records, pension and bounty land warrant applications

6125 Sand Point Way, N.E.
Seattle, WA 98115-7999
Tel: 206-336-5115
Fax:206-336-5112

National Archives—Pacific Alaska Region (Seattle):
http://www.archives.gov/seattle/

Idaho State Archives – manuscripts, personal papers, historical maps, historical newspapers, oral histories, county records, census schedules, death certificates

2205 Old Penitentiary Road
Boise, ID 83712
Tel: 208-334-3863
Fax: 208-334-2626

Idaho State Archives : http://history.idaho.gov/archives-collections

University of Idaho - Regional Depository for U.S. Government Documents for the state of Idaho, collection contains pension lists, private land claims, veterans' burial lists, historical maps, photographs and more

Rayburn Street
Moscow, ID 83844-2350
Ph. 208-885-6314
FAX 208-885-6817

University of Idaho: http://libguides.uidaho.edu/Documents

Mountain West Digital Library - central search portal for digital collections amounting to more than 800,000 resources from colleges, universities, public libraries, historical societies, museums, and government agencies, counties, and municipalities in Nevada, Idaho, Utah, Arizona, Hawaii, and other areas of the western United States

Mountain West Digital Library: http://mwdl.org/

Idaho State University - Department of Special Collections and University Archives Manuscript Collection – manuscript collection, personal papers, diaries, correspondence, business records

921 S. 8th Ave, Stop 8089
Pocatello, ID 83209-8089
Tel: 208-282-3152
Email: refdesk@isu.edu

Department of Special Collections and University Archives Manuscript Collection:
http://www.isu.edu/library/special/scmc.htm

Library of Congress in Washington, DC - Genealogy and Local History Section - large collection of manuscripts, histories, published genealogies, directories, maps, and newspapers.

101 Independence Ave. at First Street, S.E.
Washington, D.C. 20504
Tel: 202-707-5000
Fax: 202-707-5844

Genealogy and Local History Section:
http://www.loc.gov/rr/genealogy/

Brigham Young University - Idaho Library in Rexburg - access to a large collection of original research material on Eastern Idaho and Utah settlers - Upper Snake River Family History Center is hosted in the Library

McKay Library
Brigham Young University - Idaho
525 South Center St.
Rexburg, Idaho 84440-0405

Brigham Young University - Idaho Library in Rexburg:
http://www.lib.byui.edu/

Idaho Genealogical and Historical Societies

Genealogical and historical societies have access to extensive catalogues of genealogical data. They are also able to offer expert guidance for genealogical researchers. Many members are professional genealogists who are most willing to share their expertise in finding ancestors.

Idaho State Historical Society - manuscripts, personal papers, historical maps, historical newspapers, oral histories, county records, census schedules, death certificates

2205 Old Penitentiary Road
Boise, Idaho 83712
Phone 208-334-2682
Fax 208-334-2774

Idaho State Historical Society: http://history.idaho.gov/archives-collections

Idaho Genealogical Society, Inc. – county histories, historical maps, various genealogical resources
P.O. Box 1854
Boise, Idaho 83701-1854
Email Us at: idahogenealogy@hotmail.com

Idaho Genealogical Society, Inc: http://www.idahogenealogy.org/

Twin Rivers Genealogy Society – cemetery records, surname index, obituaries, photos and post cards

PO Box 386
Lewiston, ID 83501

Twin Rivers Genealogy Society:
http://www.twinriversgenealogy.org/

Idaho Family History Centers

The Family History Centers run by the LDS Church offer free access to billions of genealogical records for free to the general public. They also provide classes on genealogy and one-on-one assistance to inexperienced family historians. Here you will find a **Complete Listing of Idaho Family History Centers**.

Complete Listing of Idaho Family History Centers:
https://familysearch.org/locations/centerlocator

Additional Idaho Genealogical Resources

Idaho Mailing Lists

Mailing lists are internet based facilities that use email to distribute a single message to all who subscribe to it. When information on a particular surname, new records, or any other important genealogy information related to the mailing list topic becomes available, the subscribers are alerted to it. Joining a mailing list is an excellent way to stay up to date on Idaho genealogy research topics. Rootsweb have an extensive listing of **Idaho Mailing Lists** on a variety of topics.

Idaho Mailing Lists:
http://lists.rootsweb.ancestry.com/index/usa/ID/misc.html

Idaho Message Boards

A message board is another internet based facility where people can post questions about a specific genealogy topic and have it answered by other genealogists. If you have questions about a surname, record type, or research topic, you can post your question and other researchers and genealogists will help you with the answer. Be sure to check back regularly, as the answers are not emailed to you. The Idaho message boards at **Rootsweb** are completely free to use.

Irootsweb:
http://boards.rootsweb.com/localities.northam.usa.states/mb.ashx

Idaho Newspapers and Periodicals

Many genealogy periodicals and historical newspapers contain reprinted copies of family genealogies, transcripts of family Bible records, information about local records and archives, census indexes, church records, queries, land records, obituaries, court records, cemetery records, and wills. The following sites have historical Idaho newspapers and periodicals that you can search online or on-site.

GenealogyBank.com – free searchable database of Idaho newspaper archives, 1864-1922

GenealogyBank.com:
http://www.genealogybank.com/gbnk/newspapers/explore/USA/Idaho/

Library of Congress Digital Newspaper Directory – free searchable database of historical U.S. newspapers dating from 1690-present

Library of Congress Digital Newspaper Directory:
http://chroniclingamerica.loc.gov/search/titles/

The Online Books Page – links to historical books and periodicals available for viewing online, dating from mid-16th century

The Online Books Page: http://onlinebooks.library.upenn.edu/

NewspaperArchive.com – largest online database of historical newspapers in the world.

NewspaperArchive.com: http://newspaperarchive.com/

Historical Idaho Maps and Gazetteers

Maps are an integral part of genealogical research. They help us to locate landmarks, towns, cities, parishes, states, provinces, waterways and roads and streets. They also help us to determine when and where boundary changes might have taken place, and give us a visualization of the area we're researching in. For locating place names, a gazetteer is the best possible resource for any genealogist. Gazetteers are also sometimes called "place name dictionaries", and can help you to locate the area in which you need to conduct research. Below are links to the maps and gazetteers for research in Idaho.

Peabody GNIS Service – Idaho:
http://peabody.research.yale.edu/cgi-bin/Query.GNIS?ST=Idaho&SU=1

Color Landform Atlas – Idaho:
http://fermi.jhuapl.edu/states/id_0.html

1985 U.S. Atlas : http://www.livgenmi.com/1895/ID/

Idaho Hometown Locator: http://idaho.hometownlocator.com/

Idaho City Directories

.

City directories are similar to telephone directories in that they list the residents of a particular area. The difference though is what is important to genealogists, and that is they pre-date telephone directories. You can find an ancestor's information such as their street address, place of employment, occupation, or the name of their spouse. A one-stop-shop for finding city directories in Idaho is the **Idaho Online Historical Directories** which contains a listing of every available city and historical directory related to Idaho.

Idaho State Historical Society:
http://history.idaho.gov/sites/default/files/uploads/reference-series/0445.pdf

Idaho Online Historical Directories:
https://sites.google.com/site/onlinedirectorysite/Home/usa/id

Boise Public Library -Idaho Satesman; microfilm of the paper from 1864 to present.

715 S. Capitol Blvd.
Boise, ID 83702
(208) 384-4076

Boise Public Library: http://www.boisepubliclibrary.org/locations/

Idaho State Historical Society - City and regional directories from 1908-1990's on microfilm

2205 Old Penitentiary Road
Boise,
Idaho 83712
Phone 208-334-2682
Fax 208-334-2774

Idaho State Historical Society:
http://history.idaho.gov/sites/default/files/uploads/reference-series/0445.pdf

Idaho Genealogical Records

Birth, Death, Marriage and Divorce Records – Also known as vital records, birth, death, and marriage certificates are the most basic, yet most important records attached to your ancestor. The reason for their importance is that they not only place your ancestor in a specific place at a definite time, but potentially connect the individual to other relatives. Below is a list of repositories and websites where you can find Idaho vital records

Idaho Bureau of Vital Records and Health Statistics - birth and death records from 1911 to present, and marriage and divorce records from 1947 to the present. Some counties might have older vital records in their files, though county files are limited only to events that occurred in that county.

Idaho Bureau of Vital Records and Health Statistics:
http://healthandwelfare.idaho.gov/?TabId=82

Family Search has the following indexes that can be searched online for free.

Idaho Births and Christenings, 1856-1965:
https://familysearch.org/search/collection/1674809

Idaho, Deaths and Burials, 1907-1965:
https://familysearch.org/search/collection/1674815

Idaho Marriages, 1878-1898 and 1903-1942:
https://familysearch.org/search/collection/1674817

Idaho County Marriages, 1864-1950:
https://familysearch.org/search/collection/1662500

Census Reports

Census records are among the most important genealogical documents for placing your ancestor in a particular place at a specific time. Like BDM records, they can also lead you to other ancestors, particularly those who were living under the authority of the head of household. Idaho census records are available from 1870-1930, and there are several repositories, both online and off, where you can find them.

Census-Online – online Idaho census reports from 1870-1930

Census-Online: http://www.census-online.com/links/ID/

National Archives—Pacific Alaska Region (Seattle) – Federal census records 1870-1930

6125 Sand Point Way, N.E.
Seattle, WA 98115-7999
Tel: 206-336-5115
Fax:206-336-5112

National Archives—Pacific Alaska Region (Seattle): http://www.archives.gov/seattle/

Access Genealogy - Idaho census records from 1820-1930

Access Genealogy: http://www.accessgenealogy.com/census/idaho-census-records.htm

African American Census Schedules Online – slave schedules, mortality schedules, slave-owners census

African American Census Schedules Onlin: http://www.afrigeneas.com/aacensus/ga/

Native Americans in Census Records (US National Archives)

Native Americans in Census Records: http://www.archives.gov/research/census/native-americans/

Idaho Church Records

Church and synagogue records are a valuable resource, especially for baptisms, marriages, and burials that took place before 1900. You will need to at least have an idea of your ancestor's religious denomination, and in most cases you will have to visit a brick and mortar establishment to view them.

Most church records are kept by the individual church, although in some denominations, records are placed in a regional archive or maintained at the diocesan level. Local Historical Societies are sometimes the repository for the state's older church records. Below are links archives that maintain church records, as well as a few databases that can be viewed online.

The **Family History Library** contains many church records from a variety of denominations on microfilm.

The **Idaho State Archives** has a significant collection of Episcopal church records and an index to Catholic records

The **Augustana College Library** in Rock Island Illinois has a multi-denominational collection of Idaho church records including Evangelical, Baptist, Lutheran, and Covenant.

Family History Library:
http://familysearch.org/learn/wiki/en/Family_History_Library

Idaho State Archives: http://history.idaho.gov/idaho-state-archives

Augustana College Library: http://www.augustana.edu/general-information/swenson-center-/genealogy/church-records/idaho---indiana

Central Repositories for Denominational Records

Most of the records of individual denominations are kept in central repositories. Below is a list of the major congregational archives for Idaho with links to their websites, physical addresses, and contact information.

LDS

LDS Church History Library (Archives)
15 East North Temple
Salt Lake City, UT 84150
Telephone: (801) 240-2272
Fax: (801) 240-1845

LDS Church History Library (Archives):
http://churchhistorylibrary.lds.org

Methodist

United Methodist Archives Center
Drew University
36 Madison Ave.
Madison, NJ 07940-4007
Tel: (973) 408-3125
Fax: (973) 408-3770

United Methodist Archives Center: http://www.gcah.org/

Presbyterian

The Presbyterian Historical Society
425 Lombard Street
Philadelphia, PA 19147-1516
Tel: (215) 627-1852
Fax: (215) 627-0509

The Presbyterian Historical Society: http://www.history.pcusa.org/

<u>Roman Catholic</u>

Diocese of Boise
303 Federal Way
Boise, ID 83705
Phone: (208) 342-1311
Fax: (208) 342-0224

Diocese of Boise:
http://www.catholicidaho.org/en/Pages/RCDBhome.aspx

Idaho Military Records

More than 40 million Americans have participated in some time of war service since America was colonized. The chance of finding your ancestor amongst those records is exceptionally high. Military records can even reveal individuals who never actually served, such as those who registered for the two World Wars but were never called to duty.

Below are a number of links to websites and archives that contain Idaho military records.

U.S. National Archives – WWI Draft registration cards, casualties lists, WWI and WWII service records, Korean War records, Vietnam War records, Civil War and Spanish-American War records, and casualties lists.

U.S. National Archives:
http://www.archives.gov/research/military/veterans/online.html

United States Index to Indian Wars Pension Files, 1892-1926 – military pension records of soldiers who fought in the Indian Wars between 1817 and 1898

United States Index to Indian Wars Pension Files, 1892-1926:
https://familysearch.org/search/collection/1979427

United States Registers of Enlistments in the U.S. Army, 1798-1914 - index of men who enlisted in the United States Army, 1798-1914.

United States Registers of Enlistments in the U.S. Army, 1798-1914: https://familysearch.org/search/collection/1880762

United States Mexican War Pension Index, 1887-1926 - index to Mexican War pension files for service between 1846 and 1848

United States Mexican War Pension Index, 1887-1926:
https://familysearch.org/search/collection/1979390

Civil War Soldiers Service Records - Service records for both Union and Confederate soldiers indexed by soldier's name, rank, and unit.

Civil War Soldier Service Records:
http://go.fold3.com/civilwar_records/

Idaho Cemetery Records

As convenient as it is to search cemetery records online, keep in mind that there are a few disadvantages over visiting a cemetery in person. They are:

- Tombstone information is not always accurately transcribed
- The arrangement of the graves in a cemetery can be crucial as family members are often buried next to each other or in the same grave. This arrangement is not always preserved in the alphabetical indexes that are found online.

With that information in mind, the following websites have databases that can be searched online for Idaho Cemetery records.

Idaho Tombstone Transcription Project - death and burial records

Idaho Tombstone Transcription Project:
http://www.usgwtombstones.org/idaho/idaho.html

African American Cemeteries Online – African American, slave, and Native American cemetery records

African American Cemeteries Online:
http://africanamericancemeteries.com/

Access Genealogy – huge database of Idaho cemetery record transcriptions

Access Genealogy:
http://www.accessgenealogy.com/cemetery/idaho-cemetery-records.htm

Find a Grave – over 100 million grave records can be searched on this site. Search can be conducted by name, location, or cemetery name.

Find a Grave: http://www.findagrave.com/

Interment.net - A free online database containing approximately 4 million cemetery records from around the world.

Interment.net: http://www.interment.net/

Billion Graves – as the name implies, you can search a billion records including headstone photos, transcriptions, cemetery records, and grave locations.

Billion Graves:
http://billiongraves.com/pages/search/index.php#cemetery

Idaho Obituaries

Obituaries can reveal a wealth about our ancestor and other relatives. You can search our **Idaho Newspaper Obituaries Listings** from hundreds of Idaho newspapers online for free.

Idaho Newspaper Obituaries Listings:
http://obituarieshelp.org/idaho_newspaper_obituaries.html

Idaho Wills and Probate Records

The documents found in a probate packet may include a complete
inventory of a person's estate, newspaper entries, witness testimony,
a copy of a will, list of debtors and creditors, names of executors or
trustees, names of heirs. They can not only tell you about the
ancestor you're currently researching, but lead to other ancestors.
Most of these records must be accessed at a county court or clerk's
office, but some can be found online as well. You can obtain copies
of the original probate records by writing to the county clerk.

Idaho County Courthouses Directory

Idaho County Courthouses Directory:
http://isc.idaho.gov/files/county_courthouse_directory.pdf

Idaho Counties - Will Testators Indexes

Idaho Counties - Will Testators Indexes :
http://sampubco.com/wills/id/idaho.htm

Idaho State Archives – early case files

2205 Old Penitentiary Road
Boise, ID 83712
Tel: 208-334-3863
Fax: 208-334-2626

Idaho State Archives: http://history.idaho.gov/archives-collections

Family History Library - a few published volumes of probate
records and some microfilmed early estate indexes and will registers.

Family History Library:
http://familysearch.org/learn/wiki/en/Family_History_Library

Idaho Immigration and Naturalization Records

The naturalization process generated many types of records, including petitions, declarations of intention, and oaths of allegiance. These records can provide family historians with information such as a person's birth date and place of birth, immigration year, marital status, spouse information, occupation, witnesses' names and addresses, and more.

Idaho State Historical Society – county and state level naturalization records

2205 Old Penitentiary Road
Boise, Idaho 83712
Phone 208-334-2682
Fax 208-334-2774

Idaho State Historical Society:
http://www.history.idaho.gov/naturalization

US National Archives – Immigration and Naturalization records for the entire United States

US National Archives:
http://www.archives.gov/research/immigration/passenger-arrival.html

Family Search – naturalizations and citizenship records dating from 1789

Family Search:
https://familysearch.org/search/catalog/results#count=20&query=%2Bsubject_id%3A505381

The **Oregon-California Trails Association** is an organization that promotes the story of the westward migration to Idaho. Their site includes a personal name index to trail diaries, autobiographies, newspaper articles, journals, reminiscences, guidebooks, and letters.

Oregon-California Trails Association: http://www.octa-trails.org/

Idaho Native American Records

Access Genealogy – Idaho Native American census records, tribal histories, and much more

Access Genealogy: http://www.accessgenealogy.com/native/north-dakota-indian-tribes.htm

U.S. National Archives - information on American Indians who maintained their ties to Federally-recognized Tribes (1830-1970).

U.S. National Archives: http://www.archives.gov/research/native-americans/

Records of the Bureau of Indian Affairs (BIA): **http://www.archives.gov/research/guide-fed-records/groups/075.html**

American Indians Records Repository - records dating from the 1700s including trust, education and other historic Indian Affairs records

American Indian Records Repository
Meritex Enterprises
17501 West 98th Street
Lenexa, KS 66219
Phone: 913-888-0601

American Indians Records Repository:
http://www.doi.gov/ost/records_mgmt/american-indian-records-repository.cfm

Missing Matriarchs – Resources for Researching Female Idaho Ancestors

Looking for female ancestors requires an adjustment of how we view traditional records sources. A woman's identity was often under that of her husband, and often individual records for them can be difficult to locate. The following resources are effective in locating female ancestors in Idaho where traditional records may not reveal them.

Marriage and Divorce Records

County clerks have recorded marriages since 1860. **Brigham Young University–Idaho** in Rexburg has marriage indexes to 1900 in their Special Collections. County district courts have jurisdiction over divorces and official registration began in 1947. Some County records have been filmed such as:

- Oneida County Court marriages 1865-1941, index 1865-1976, and certificates, 1887-1895 (film 1450637 ff.)
- Oneida County Court calendar including divorces, 1874-1879 (film 1502903) and court records 1879-1884 (film 1450649 ff.) at the Oneida County Courthouse in Malad

Brigham Young University–Idaho:
http://abish.byui.edu/specialCollections/famhist/index.cfm

Bibliographies

- *Idaho Folklife: Homesteads to Headstones,* Louie W. Attebery (University of Utah Press, 1985)
- *Idaho of Yesterday,* Thomas Donaldson (The Caxton Printer, 1941)
- *Idaho Women in History,* Betty Penson-Ward (Northwest Publishing Company, 1991)
- *Idaho Ethnic Heritage,* Bobby Rahder and Mary reed (Idaho Historical Society and Idaho Centennial Commission, 1990)

Selected Resources for Idaho Women's History

McKay Library
BYU University Idaho
525 South Center
Rexburg, ID 83460-0405

University of Idaho Library
S Rayburn St Moscow
ID 83844

Common Idaho Surnames

The following surnames are among the most common in Idaho and are also being currently researched by other genealogists. If you find your surname here, there is a chance that some research has already been performed on your ancestor.

Adams, Barton, Beck, Bennett, Benton, Biggs, Binch, Bird, Boka, Brinton, Bruce, Carlson, Carter, Christensen, Clark, Constant, Cromwell, Crossgrove, Cummins, Dametz, Davis, Denney, Devitt, Dibble, Douglas, Elkin, Frost, Fuller, Gammell, Golay, Grant, Green, Hanson, Hardman, Harrison, Haymond, Hewitt, Hodson, Holley, Hudson, Ingram, Inshaw, Isaac, Jensen, Jewkes, Johnson, Jones, Kendall, King, Konold, Lamm, Land, Larsen, Leeper, Letts, Logan, Manwaring, Marlett, McDonald, Moore, Mower, Neilson, Nelson, Padfield, Perry, Rape, Redmond, Robins Scott, Scovil, Secrist, Simon, Simons, Snow, Sornsen, Summers, Thomas, Thompson, Thornley, Thurston, Tidwell, Tuckett, Van Dyke, Wall, Ware, Watson, Welker, Willardson, Williams, Young

Notes

Notes

www.ingramcontent.com/pod-product-compliance
Lightning Source LLC
Chambersburg PA
CBHW071343310526
45790CB00018B/1242